BYGONE ASHBOURNE

Lindsey Porter

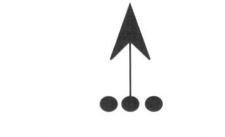

Landmark Publishing

Published by

Landmark Publishing

The Oaks, Moor Farm Road West, Ashbourne, DE6 1HD
Tel: (01335) 347349 Fax: (01335) 347303
Email: landmark@clara.net Web: www.landmarkpublishing.co.uk

1st Edition

ISBN: 978-1-84306-407-7

© **Lindsey Porter 2008**

The right of Lindsey Porter as author of this work has been asserted by him in accordance with the Copyright, Design and Patents Act, 1993.

All rights reserved. No part of this publication may be reproduced, stored in a retrieval system or transmitted in any form or by any means, electronic, mechanical, photocopying, recording or otherwise without the prior permission of Landmark Publishing Ltd.

British Library Cataloguing in Publication Data: a catalogue record for this book is available from the British Library.

Printed by: TJ International, Padstow

Captions

Front cover: Church Street before the railway was built.

Back cover top: A procession crossing the old medieval bridge at Hanging Bridge. The banner is of the National United Order of Free Gardeners.

Back cover bottom: An early view of Compton.

Page 1: Station Street prior to developement.

CONTENTS

1. The Market Place — 4
2. St. John's Street — 14
3. Church Street/Mayfield Road — 27
4. Dig Street/Compton — 39
5. Station Street/Clifton Road — 55
6. Public Houses — 65
7. The Railway — 75
8. Park Road — 82
9. Events — 85

AUTHOR'S NOTE

This book consists of a choice of photographs taken from my previous three books on Ashbourne:- The Spirit of Ashbourne Volumes 1 & 2 plus Victorian Times in and around Ashbourne.
Demand for the books has continued since they went out of print and it is eight years since the first was published. The decision to produce a compendium of some of the best from all three reflects the changed economic circumstances and a more affordable retail price.
The captions have been rewritten in most cases, incorporating research which was completed after the books were published. I have chosen not to include many scenes of Shrovetide Football, despite my obvious interest in it, other than one of Clifton Mill and where there is other interest in the scene.

ACKNOWLEDGEMENTS

I wish to thank all those who provided images used in this book. A full list appeared in the two *Spirit of Ashbourne* titles and *Victorian Ashbourne*. However most of the photographs do not bear the name of the donor and I am unable to individually attribute the images I have used.

LINDSEY PORTER

1. THE MARKET PLACE

We tend to take our Market Place for granted I suspect, it is always 'there'; its repetitive weekly market days (Thursday & Saturday) interchanging with its use as a central car park. However, over longer periods, it has changed. Its central role as a meeting place, animal and provision market has changed and so have some of its buildings since the Georgian and Victorian rebuilding of what would have been smaller buildings.

Above: this view amid carts and stalls, is towards Slater's shop and a property behind it. Slaters' were grocers and their premises are shown below, on the corner of Union Street (far left). Note the other buildings also now gone to the right of Slaters.

Here is Slater's shop again plus the white-painted building. Beyond that can just be seen the end wall of the White Horse pub next to the shop, (still there) and then the White Lion, now Bramhalls. There was quite a jumble of closely-built properties behind Slaters and the building next to it. Note the sign on the White Horse pub for Lowndes' leather shop. Fred Sellars, ballmaker, worked here until 1906 when he went to the Market Place to run his own business.

Once the old building next to Slaters was removed the properties behind came into view. To the left of them would appear to be the large building on page 13, fronting The Channel, which stood behind Slaters.

A general view of market day following the rebuilding of the two-storey building on p8. Animals were penned here or in adjacent streets for sale prior to the building of the cattle market.

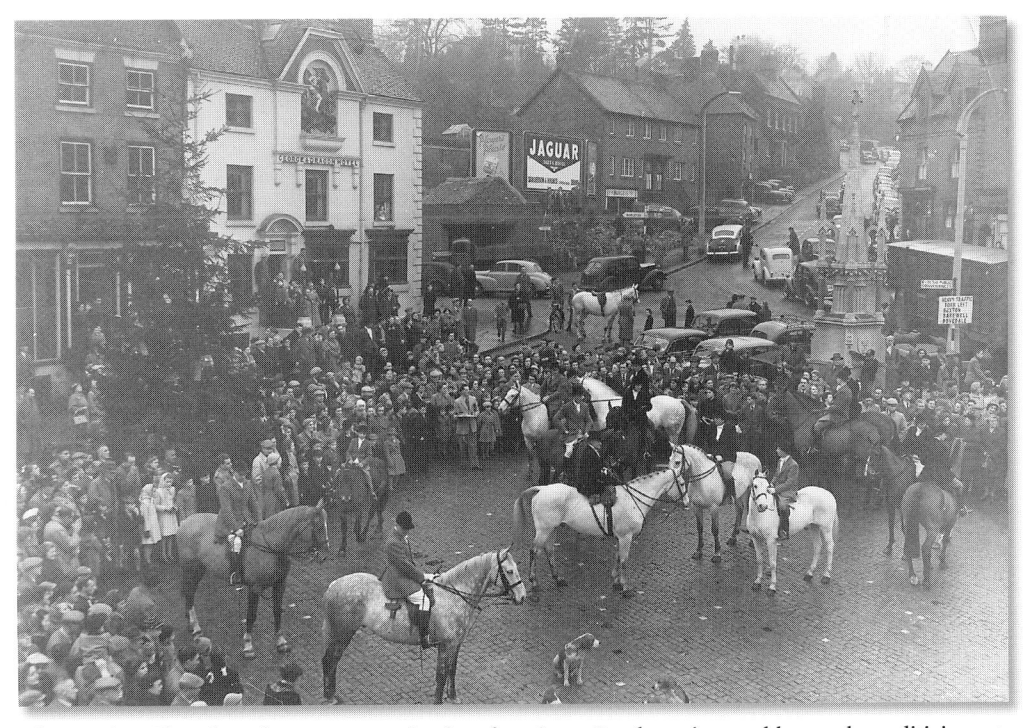

The Market Place has always attracted other functions: Proclamations, addresses by politicians etc. Here we have the local hunt seen attracting quite a crowd. Note the scene after the demolition of Slaters and adjoining properties.

Two-storey properties adjacent to Spencers, rebuilt in 1897.

This pre-1897 scene shows the two-storey building (far left) and just a few stalls hoping to attract business.

Another busier scene, showing the horse traffic in the days before the motor car.

A scene in The Butchery, now Victoria Square. The shop on the left seems to bear the name Sellers. Off to the left is the Horns pub, the name deriving from the antlers on the Duke of Devonshire's Coat of Arms. Off to the right was the Tiger Inn, now the Lamplight Restaurant. This inn closed in 1906 when the licensee was Annie Richardson. Closure was forced under The Licensing Act, 1904 as it failed to reach certain standards laid down by the Act. The Durham Ox on Compton, where Fred Arnold was the licensee, closed at the same time. The Three Horse Shoes and the Stag & Pheasant (latter in Compton) beer houses open prior to 1869, also closed in 1906. The licensees were Joseph Brown and Robert Burton respectively.

A funeral passing down the Market Place. This may have been a soldier of the Great War, but the use of a gun carriage suggests someone of greater importance. It could be that of Col. Wilkie of The Mansion, who died in December 1894, but hardly anyone is wearing a coat. It may therefore, be the funeral of Col. Jelf, who died c. 1918-20. Note the properties in Union Street and the corner of Slater's shop, all now demolished.

Wibberley's shop in the building now used as the Tourist Information Centre, next to the Ashbourne ex-Workingmen's Club. Mr Wibberley was a 'cooper & general dealer'.

A view towards Victoria Square, at the side of the Leek United Building Society. Gallimore's butchers later became Mr Hollingsworth's butchers and then when he retired was incorporated into the Horns pub. The gas lamp has also gone but the wooden feature on the right remains.

Above: Demolished properties in Union Street.

Left: Another property now gone. The toilets remain, but the other buildings have been demolished. Note the bottom of The Channel.

2. ST. JOHN'S STREET

A lovely scene at the corner with Dig Street and Church Street. The Wheatsheaf Hotel has been converted to the bank. Next door, Neals tobacconist and a house with a bay window occupy the site of Dorothy Perkins shop. Next to that was the timber-framed barbers shop, now Bookthrift, in a later building. The River Plate Meat Co occupied the now removed building behind the horse and cart. To the right of it is a sweet shop. The lack of cars suggests a date pre-1895. On the right corner is Cash & Co's clothing shop. A man strolls up the street with a wheelbarrow. It all looks very Victorian, but it isn't! The Green Man Hotel sign is advertising "Garage & Petrol".

Left: The reverse view, showing the building on the site of Bookthrift. Note the gas lamps for lighting the street.

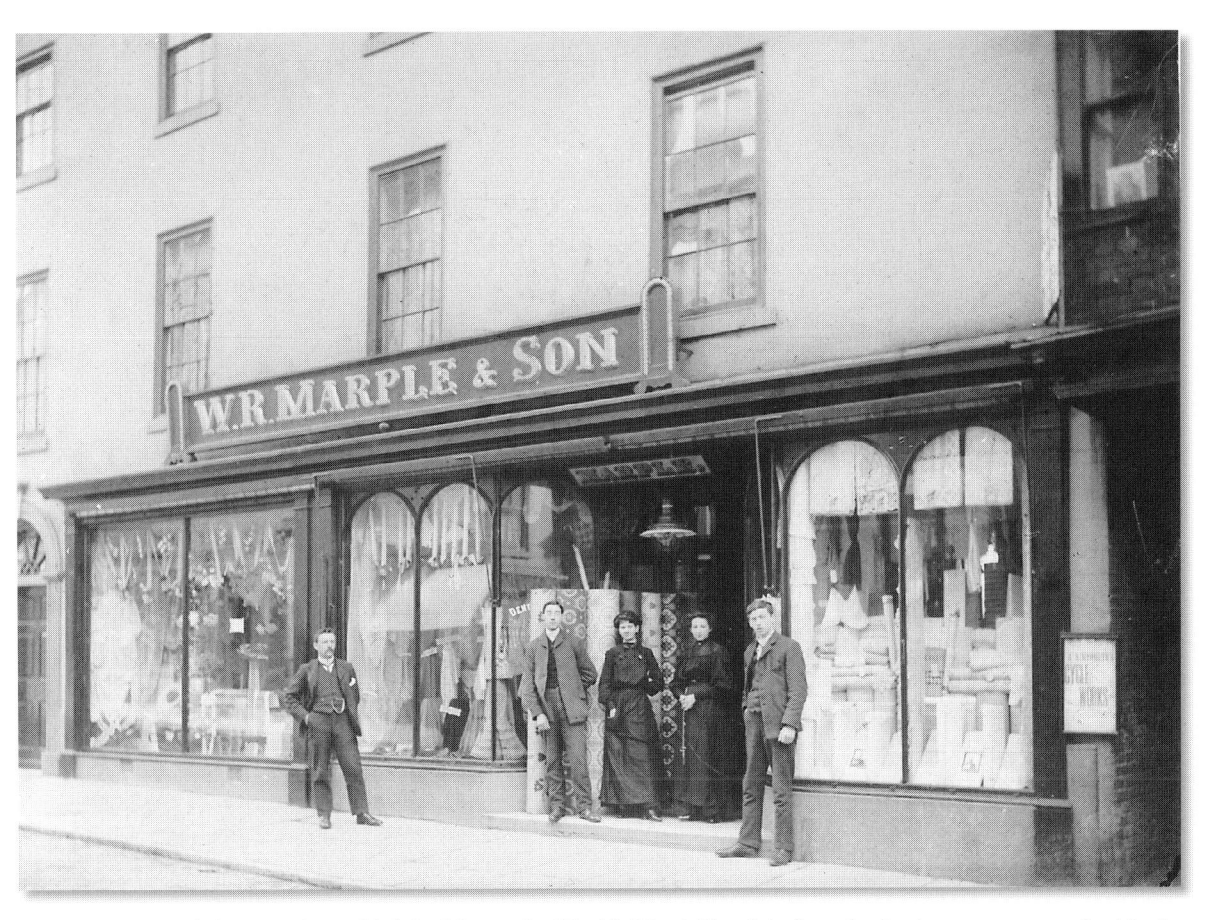

Marples occupied the premises which had been the Black's Head Hotel, before the business was merged with the Green Man Hotel. The entry on the right was where Redvers Wibberley had his painting business about 80 years ago. Despite the passage of time, his sign, painted on the wall of the entry, still survives in good condition.

Another view of the beginning of St John Street. The first shop is Skellenn's grocers, advertising soap and starch. Note the barber's pole. His sign says 'Pool. Hair cutter'. Nothing about hair styling in those days. In The Butchery/Victoria Square is the antlers sign and what looks like the name Duke of Devonshire (?Arms). It later became the Stag's Horns and now of course, is the The Horns. The Wellington Inn in St John Street, currently closed, was previously known as the Duke of Devonshire.

The Green Man Hotel, when Fanny Wallis was the licensee, which dates the photograph to 1898 (when she died) or earlier. The near right building was already a bank. Up the street one can make out the inn sign for the Horse & Jockey, which closed in 1899. Fanny Wallis took over the Green Man in the 1840s with Robert Wallis her husband. He permitted use of Shaw Croft when the Market Place Shrovetide turn-up was banned in 1863. This is how the Green Man became the game's 'spiritual' home (in more senses than one). Fanny was the daughter of John Wheeldon, one of three central people on the 1862 Shrovetide painting.

A close up of Mr Osbournes shop before his son entered the business (see p.18).

A similar view showing a busier day. A horse plods up the street pulling a loaded cart and a bus waits for passengers.

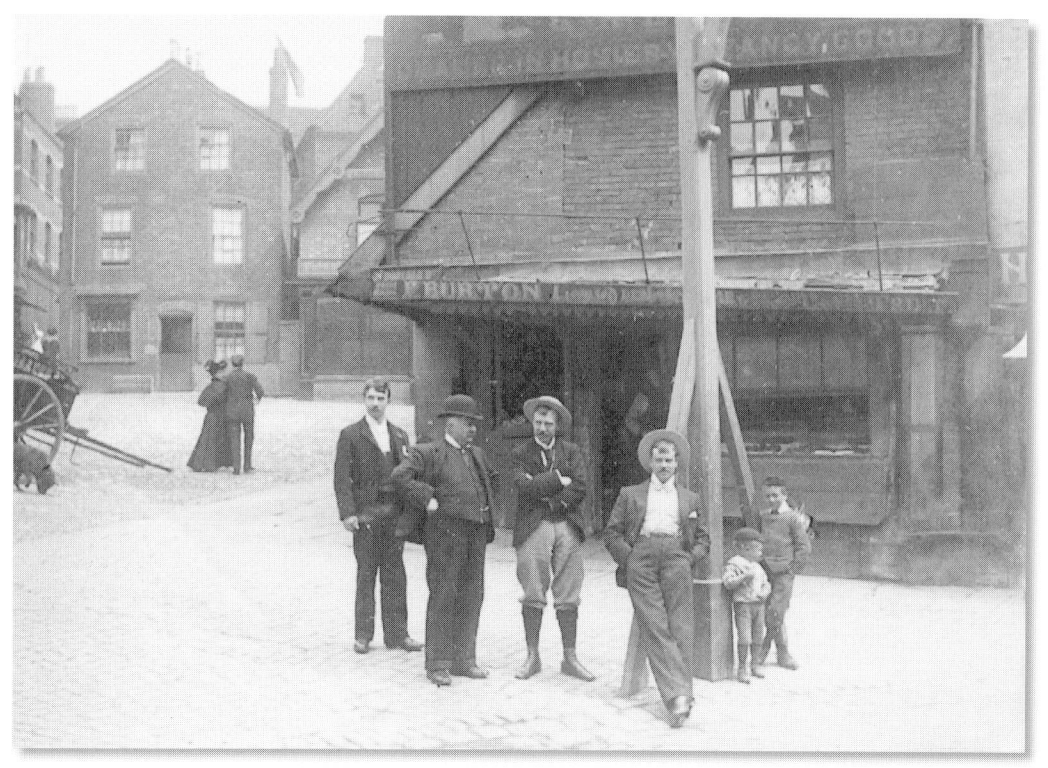

The bottom of Victoria Square. The building on the right has been replaced. Note the absence of the mounting block.

A quiet day in the street. Mr Osbourne had taken on the shop on the right (now WH Smith). He founded the Ashbourne News newspaper in 1890 and traded here as J Osbourne (later adding '& Son'). The sweet shop still carries the Fry's Chocolate sign plus a much larger one saying 'Restaurant' which was perhaps upstairs. The Horse & Jockey Inn sign has gone (therefore the scene is post-1899).

The first scene in this book showing cyclists, it is taken from the top of Horse & Jockey Yard.

Howell & Marsden's grocers shop opposite the Green Man. Presumably the boxes and barrels on p.18 above were a delivery to here. This was one of the most respected grocers in the town. They obviously knew a thing or two about window displays. The business later became Bagnalls.

Mr Bradley's shop. The building on the left features on the scene on p.21 (bottom) and is now Young Ideas.

A 1950s scene, again from the Horse & Jockey Yard entrance. The buildings on the right had a major refurbishment, which saved them from demolition. The girder projecting from the window is a reminder that the upstairs was shored-up internally. Dewhurst's started in Ashbourne in the 1930s.

It would be nice to know more about this scene. People are standing and watching, but if it was the Carnival would there have been more on the street? The Red Lion Inn is boarded up and the shop behind the ladders (Bradley's) is empty too.

Bradley's shop may have been taken by the Co-op (see far right). The main building in this scene has been demolished, the site being occupied by the cabin for older residents of the town. The shop was a greengrocers and florist.

The Co-op Society.

Woolworth's shop being boarded up for Shrovetide.

A more recent scene showing Boots prior to their move to Shaw Croft.

A view back down the street. The 'To Let' signs are visible again on the right (opposite top photograph). Smith's Tavern was then Smith & Son, wholesale wine and spirit merchants. A sign 'God Save the King' perhaps points towards 1901 or 1911.

The upper part of the street showing the entrance gate to Ashbourne Hall.

The building on the right is now The Gingerbread Shop, but here its timber framing is hidden behind plaster.

The upper part of the street on Diamond Jubilee Day, 1897. Note the tables on the pavement, for a street party later on. The use of arches and garlands across the streets was not confined to national celebrations. They happened at other events too. At the local society wedding of the Rev. F.C.R. Jourdain (the vicar of Clifton and the eldest son of the vicar of Ashbourne) and Miss Frances E. Smith of Clifton House, Clifton, arches and garlands were hung across the streets in celebration. The wedding was in July 1896. The church bells were often used to mark important people passing through the town.

Ashbourne Hall, 1887, with members of the Frank family.

Another view of the Hall. The oldest surviving part of the building would appear to be the entrance, which was the original stairwell and has a (? Jacobean) ribbed vaulting to the ground floor ceiling.

The former Hall stables in Cokayne Avenue, when used as a highways depot. They have now been converted into apartments.

3. CHURCH STREET AND MAYFIELD ROAD

A close up of a lovely horse standing patiently with its cart at the junction of Church Street and St John Street.

The view into Church Street, before the White Hart was reduced in width and whilst the Wheatsheaf Hotel (right) was still in use.

A close up of Corner House shop windows.

The Corner House shop, 1953 with Coronation bunting.

Lightbody, Bingham & Co were tailors and shoe sellers, situated opposite Corner House.

The shop in the previous picture is above the horse in this view. This scene shows The White Hart before the buildings over the arch were removed. The shop this side the arch is Bass & Co off-licence. The pub sign advertises 'horse & carriage for hire'. What is the contraption on the pavement in front of the off-licence – or is it a couple of cases? Beyond Corner House is Coates who appear to be milliners.

A horse-drawn sledge coming down the street.

Properties demolished to make way for the junction of Station Road and Church Street. The building set back is the Methodist Church.

Houses opposite the Methodist Church together with the Old Bear Inn & The Britannia Inn beyond it. Note the cobbles in the pavement. These still remain outside the old Grammar School.

Evening meal in the Old Grammar School, c. 1951. Peter Jennings House/Classics Master is nearest the camera. In the middle of the photograph, and under the middle window, is Mr Kimmings headmaster, with his wife on the right hand side. The boys are at the near end of the room and all the girls at the other end.

Church Walk, most of this was removed for road widening.

The church interior showing the two former galleries.

Looking up the inside of the 212ft spire.

A rare view of the former west window which existed between 1840-81. It also shows the western end of Church Walk and the view towards The Paddock.

Looking down the nave towards the 1840-81 west window. This scene also shows the steps up to the south aisle gallery, removed in the 1881-82 alterations to the church.

The gas works. The last building (offices) before the former petrol station survives. The metal framing housed the gasometer, the large tank which housed the gas. It floated up and down in water inside a brick tank buried in the ground.

A close up of the gas works buildings. The petrol station appears to be selling National petrol, but I may be wrong.

A road roller parked up near the foot of Dark Lane.

A traction engine pulling three wagons of milk churns into town.

The Vicarage, off Dark Lane.

Another view of the western end of Church Walk, the shop appears to be selling groceries.

4. DIG STREET AND COMPTON

The top of Dig Street at the time of the Golden Jubilee of HM The Queen, 1887. The building on the right is The Cock Inn. Note the row of coloured glass jars on metal supports. These would have taken a small candle each to give a row of coloured lights. One wonders if the gentleman outside the pub is John Winterton. He was the landlord a few years later and probably the first Chairman of the Shrovetide Committee. He turned up a ball in 1892 and died in 1907, aged 52 years. The people on the bridge are not watching the Shrovetide game, as the Queen's Jubilee celebration was on 21st June. Was a ball turned up in honour of the event? This happened when the Princess Royal was married on 25th January 1858 and a ball was turned up in the Market Place on that day.

Another view of The Cock Inn.

The cycle shop adjacent Compton Bridge. The view below shows this property prior to conversion.

Compton Bridge and the old course of the river. Note The Terrace, the cottages on the site of The Health Centre, built in 1971-3. The field on the left is Shaw Croft. Notice the cottages across the road (right of picture).

Shrovetide Football in the old course of the river. Note The Terrace at the top left. The advert hoardings were a prominent feature of the street. The lower view is towards the Green Man Garage.

Dig Street & Compton.

Kennings Garage replaced Joseph Harrison's Green Man Garage, seen here during a flood. The river was culverted to alleviate this problem.

Kennings kept the old Green Man Garage behind the new frontage, as can be seen in this Shrovetide photograph of 1975.

Shrovetide supporters entering Shaw Croft from the side of The Terrace and Compton Bridge. The building in the middle of the picture still exists but has a new frontage. It is the Police Station.

The Terrace, at the bridge end. The first floor was a lodging house for a time.

The Terrace, showing the middle and southern end (above and below).

This property stood on the site of the Compton entrance to Sainsbury's store. The building to the right hand side was the Durham Ox Inn, now Benny's Pizza. The pub was the home of Luke Faulkner, who holds the ball on the 1862 Shrovetide painting. He was one of the last men to bait a bull in Britain.

The old Wesleyan Methodist chapel of 1822 which was on the site of the housing association flats adjacent to the Health Centre. It was later used as a wood store by Birch's Builders Yard before the site was redeveloped with sheltered housing.

Atkey's Garage was two doors along from H Smith's grocer's shop in Compton.

This property was to the left of that at the top of p.46.

Formerly part of Cooper's factory, this building was demolished to create the delivery area to Sainsburys. The first assembly line for corset manufacture was apparently in this building.

Malbon's Yard, off the west side of Compton.

Properties on the west side of Old Hill, at the end of Compton.

A view along Compton showing The Terrace on the right. The three-dormered building on the left has also gone and is now the site of the dental practice.

Atkey's Garage was later used by Dawson Macdonald & Dawson.

A view along Compton before the slight bend was removed by demolishing the properties on the right.

Many former properties can be identified by a careful study of this scene of Compton and Coopers Factory.

This old building on the car park site adjacent to the bus station must have been part of Hall's Coach Works, where carriages were made. It was in use by the fire brigade before the move to Park Road. King Edward Street was opened for traffic in 1901 but the Urban District Council objected to it and took the owners to the High Court the following year.

The old Empire Theatre with its owner Edgar Stebbings, holding the 1914 Shrovetide ball. The cinema, which opened in 1912, had seating for 650 people.

Part of Coopers H-block building and the Barnesware building affected by flooding. Sainsbury's is now on this site.

The former bowling green of Ashbourne Bowling Club, adjacent to the bus station, with the H. Block off centre left of the scene.

A lovely scene showing the Jubilee celebrations of 1887. This arch was clearly quite substantial. Note the inn signs for The Cross Keys (left) and The Roebuck (right). The Dog & Partridge Inn is the first building on the left.

5. STATION STREET AND CLIFTON ROAD

Left: This timber-framed property with a thatched roof apparently existed near North Leys. Today it would have been carefully restored instead of being swept away.

Below: Coopers staff beneath 1953 Coronation bunting in Station Street, these buidings have been swept away.

The Cooper's H-block, 1988. A proposal to convert to flats came to nothing and Sainsbury's store is now on the site. The bricks were salvaged by the Hawarden Brick Co.

The corset factory was the largest employer in the town as this top floor of the H-block shows. This view suggests that between 80-100 ladies were employed on this floor.

Another view on the top floor of the H-block.

Hoardings on the then vacant plot opposite the former Primitive Methodist Chapel. The houses behind the hoarding have now gone. They may be also seen on p.51 at the top of the scene.

The 'Prims' were founded by Hugh Bourne at Mow Cop in 1810. Many of the buildings were closed after the primitive Methodists merged with the Wensleyan Methodists.

Another view of the land opposite the chapel, looking towards South Street. The building behind The Mart van has been demolished.

The junction of Station Road and Station Street, prior to demolition of three cottages on the left hand side. Seeing a mass of people outside the railway station from this point during WWII a USA army colonel offered his assistance at what he thought was a railway accident. He was politely told it was a game of football. His reaction was not recorded.

An interesting view of the town from North Leys. The railway station is on the far left. The chimney, mid-right, was believed to be Hall's Carriage Works on the current site of the bus station.

A sight like this must have been common in the days gone by. There must have been a lot of horses stabled in the town.

The rear of Frank Wright's mill in Mayfield Road close to what was the bottom of School Lane.

The Paddock alongside Clifton Road that occupied most of the land south of the river from the rear of properties fronting Compton down to at least the North Staffordshire Railway Station. It seems to have been acquired by a Company endeavouring to release potential income from its recreational use. This view must have been from School Lane looking towards Compton. We take the annual fair for granted and it is the successor of Wombwell's Circus and the 'pleasure' fair which was held on the Paddock. In 1906, gondalas and a bywheel were to be seen for the first time.

The former goods shed on the North Stafford Railway. Locos could run through it, presumably before Jones's Corn Mill (later Frank Wright) was constructed.

The former Nestle site. The cottage (right) was removed in order to straighten the road. The factory was built on the former town tip.

Another view of the factory.

A lovely scene of bygone days at the ford Green Lane, Clifton with a girl collecting water from the river.

Clifton Mill. At long last an image of the mill has 'surfaced'. Thanks to Mrs Harrison who lent it to me and Peter Mellor for bringing it into my office for scanning. It was demolished in 1967. Clifton Mill, demolished in 1967 with the mill-house.

6. PUBLIC HOUSES

The Wheatsheaf Hotel, now remodelled as the Nat West Bank. Shrovetiders recalling the 1821 poem which refers to a beer called Warin's "tear-brain" are looking at what had been Mr Warin's inn.

The Old Bear in Church Street. This inn was sold in 1897 to Messrs Eadie, brewers of Burton on Trent. Four years later they built the Station Hotel. Some of the properties to the left were demolished to make way for the railway line to Buxton.

Another property demolished in Church Street. The building above the arch was demolished adjacent to the White Hart.

The Duke of York, which stood where the filling station with the same name is now on Mayfield Road. The light advertises Double Diamond beer, made by Ind Coope of Burton on Trent.

The Queen's Arms, at Hanging Bridge now apartments. The licensee of the Royal Oak at the other end of the bridge was shot by Scottish rebels in Bonnie Prince Charlie's army, in 1745. Humphrey Brown of Clifton was also shot and killed for refusing to hand over his horse. (Ash. News 25/10/1901) The building on the far right was a cheese factory.

Another view of the Queen's Arms, this time from the medieval road bridge before it was widened.

The Coach & Horses, Dig Street, prior to it being rebuilt.

The Durham Ox pub, now Benny's Pizza. It closed in 1906.

The view down Compton with the Dog & Partridge Inn on the left (now the Social Club).

The Machine Inn, Sturston Road, situated just before Park Road junction was an Ind Coope house. It was named after a weighing machine.

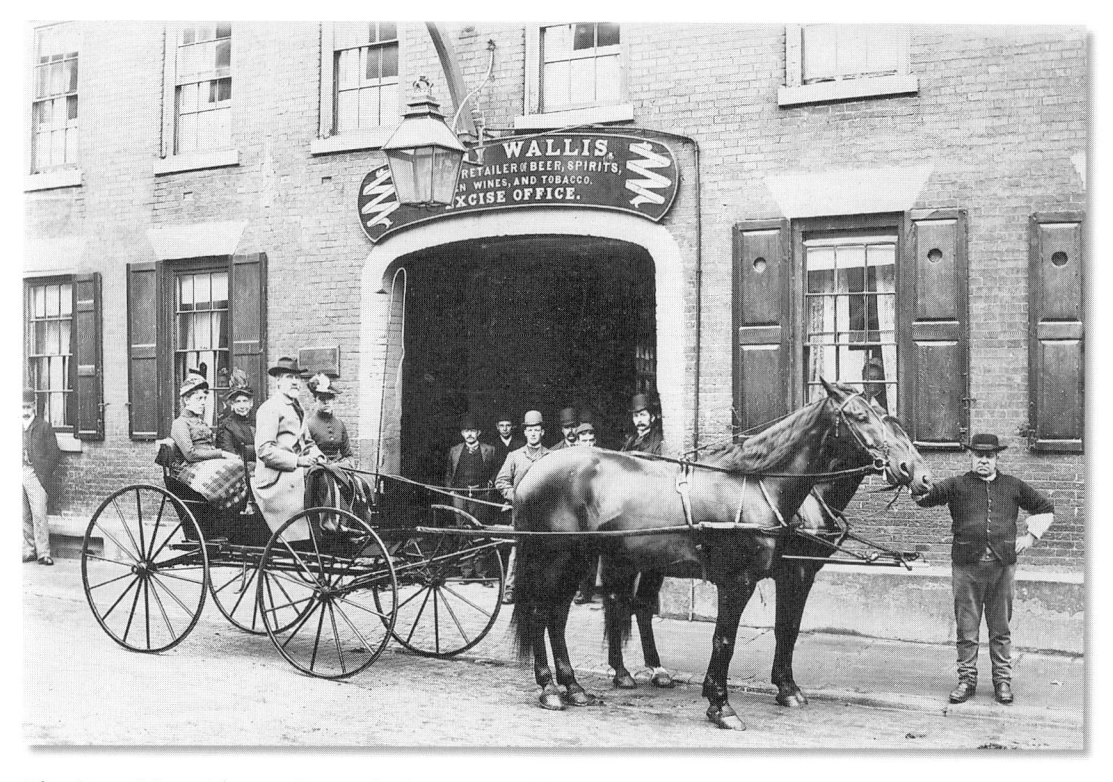

The Green Man with a carriage and pair. Fanny Wallis the licensee died in 1898 and hence the photograph is prior to then. The pipe to the right of the arch is the gas supply to the arch lamp. The gentleman with the top hat under the arch is probably Robert Wallis, Fanny's son.

Here is Fanny, albeit a poor view of her, in the Green Man Yard. She was 64 years old when she died.

Another view of the Green Man Yard when houses existed on the left side.

The Red Lion Inn at Middle Cale. Lucy Ann Blake was the licensee when the lower photograph was taken.

Ye Olde Vaults, Market Place, with The Swan on the left. The licensee when this scene was taken was named Orme. Jack Hawsworth was the licensee here when he died in 1936. He was the Shrovetide Committee Secretary for 28 years and died aged 62 years. He appears on many Shrovetide scenes in the years he was secretary. He raised a huge amount of money for charity, possibly unrivalled in the area in his day. He is buried by the path a few yards east of the south porch of St Oswald's Church. This year would appear to be the centenary of his appointment as Committee Secretary.

The Malthouse, Union Street. There were several malthouses in Ashbourne; this may have been the largest.

The White Horse Inn at the bottom of Buxton Road, the new(ish) houses were built just below Bramhalls. In the White Horse Yard, which is probably the yard portrayed on p.6, the Moon family were living in desperate conditions in 1890. Police Supt. Burford appealed for bedding for the family. The mother was in the workhouse (now the hospital) owing to infirmity and the current bedding was 'old, dirty and unfit for use'. £2.4.6d was raised (£2.22½p) for the house to be cleansed, whitewashed and all the beds and linen to be replaced. Mr Thomas Edge of Dig Street gave a bed and mattresses and Woodisse & Desborough gave a pair of mattresses. No wonder Supt. Burford was a much respected figure of authority in the town.

A wonderful scene of a wedding party, not at the White Horse Inn, but at the White Lion, two doors up the street.

7. RAILWAY

The original North Stafford Station in School Lane, partly obscured by the house on the corner of Mayfield Road. Note the lack of development in Belle Vue Road and The Paddock to the right.

The reverse view to the above, with the Railway Commercial Hotel behind. One of the Paddock gates is in the left foreground. The scene is taken from the river bridge in School Lane.

The men have their backs to the station with shop stalls to their left. The advertisement is for Gulliver's Aeriated Waters.

The railway extension to Buxton in 1890 saw a new station in a new street (Station Road) and of course the extension of the line across School Lane. The road was closed and a footbridge erected for pedestrians. This scene is well known as it shows the constructor's engine for the Buxton line behind the footbridge. The new station had an over-bridge to reach the line up to Buxton. The station site is now the swimming bath car park. The new surgery sits across the site of School Lane.

A closer view of the station that shows Compton Carriage Works and Thomas Hall & Co's sawmill. They were established, apparently in the 18th century. These buildings may well have also been the warehouse for the hundreds of copper billets (generally called 'cakes') that were brought from the Duke of Devonshires smelter at Whiston. They mainly went on by Rivercraft from Derby to Gainsborough. The copper, from Ecton Copper mine ore, was loaded at the latter port onto the SS Ecton and sailed to a warehouse where billingsgate Fish Market, London, was later built. The Ashbourne copper warehouse was in Compton.

Joseph Harrison, of King Edward Street, furniture and goods removers, had there own containers which were carried on flat railway wagons.

A view of the 1890 station. It was built of wood for cheapness. Note the gas lamps along the platforms. The four arches visible still survive which enables you to work out where the lines ran. Note the cross-over bridge and churns stacked on the down (right hand) line.

North of the tunnel were the seven arches over the Sow Brook. This structure collapsed during 'conversion' to a footpath. There was a lot of muttering as to whether the accident had been engineered or not but culpability was denied. Here are three of the arches prior to the collapse.

A view just north of the tunnel showing construction of the Buxton Line.

A traction engine pulling a small loco to start work at the end of the proposed tunnel. This is the same loco on p.76 Today we use JCBs or the like, a century ago you used locos and wagons to construct major civil engineering work.

A temporary bridge over the lane from Sandybrook to Thorpe before the brick bridge there today was constructed.

Clifton Station. The entrance to the mill was on the far left hand side and is just visible in the bottom corner. The lovely appearance of the brickwork was lost when the station was painted maybe 15 or so years ago. The signal box next to the crossing survives at Consall Station on the Churnet Valley Line. The engine is on the down line to Uttoxeter.

A goods train at Clifton Station and the signal box on the right. This station closed in the 1960s. The GPO post box at the Ashbourne Station was saved by Fred Elliot and survives at the Town Hall under lock and key.

Another train, this time on the up-line to Buxton at Ashbourne.

8. PARK ROAD

The Bath House in a much narrower Park Road. The gateway gave access to the park of Ashbourne Hall.

The Bath House in Park Road prior to demolition.

These warehouses and storage buildings adjacent to the Bath House in Park Road were demolished to makeway for housing.

Ashbourne Schoolboy's Cup Final, 1935. It is shows the Bath House in the background as it was originally constructed.

This building existed on the Sturston Road side of the junction with Park Road. It was replaced with the house below. It was the home of Peter Birch the builder, who built Peter Street. This has now also been demolished, a couple of years ago.

9. EVENTS

Finalists in the Fancy Dress Competition at a Garden Party at the Mansion House, 1953. From left: Diana Walker; ?, ?, Rosemary Cundy, Raymond & Margaret Chadwick, ?

Ashbourne Methodist School, 1956-57 (Mr Smith's class)

Two views (above and below) from the same photograph with the Derby Road area Coronation party attendees, at Ashbourne Secondary School, 1953.

Entry from Miss Sinfield's 'Sunbeam Bank' in King Street, c. 1915 Carnival. G W Walker is the boy in the left hand corner.

Ashbourne Carnival by The Terrace.

John & Cynthia Shemilt and their family took the Carnival first prize in 1954 and again in 1956. Here they are with "Over the Garden Wall". Left to right are Cynthia, Joyce Fielding, Loretta Astle, Jenny, Margaret and John.

"The King of the Hareem" was the first prize winner in the 1950 Carnival. The King was Tom Shemilt, seen here with Maisie Brown (standing). Attending on the King are Joyce Fielding, Judy Benson, Molly Clowes and three year old Maggie Shemilt.

The impressively attired Wakebourne Bank in the 1955 Carnival on Compton Bridge.

An aerial view of Church Street in 1887 from the roof of The Mansion.

Ashbourne's open-air swimming pool on Belle Vue Road.

Ashbourne Town football team, cupwinners in 1905 Joe (Ninety) Burton is in the left corner, front row.

Ashbourne Scouts c. 1919.

The Grammar School, c. 1918-19.

The Methodist School Choir, 1957-58. Shown are:

Back Row (left to right): Gill Sellors, Delia Brown, Pam Mottram, Dorothea Sandall, Peter Wilson, Adrian Smith, Diana Walker, Judith Hatton, Richard Lockyer, Bernice Dakin, Lorraine Burston.

Middle Row (left to right): Mr. Warren, Bill Featherstone, Pamela Knowles, Rosemary Pawlson, Joan Windle, Diane Hudson, Alan Bawels, Philip Hunt, Mr Hibbert.

Front Row (left to right): Gill Mears, Judith Ponsonby, Jeanette Smith, Brian Millward, Anita Spencer, David Warren, Dinah Peel, Ruth Chadwick, Gerald Vandenburg.

Mr Kennedy and the St Oswald's Bible Class in the mid 1920s. There are 48 people shown here.

St Oswold's Bible Class under Mr Weatheral c.1928-29.

A procession in 1897 leaves the Market Place on the Diamond Jubilee celebrations of HM The Queen.

The Co-optimist's Dance Band. On the piano is Wal Froggatt. The drummer is thought to be Charles Walker. Taken in the 1930s.

Another view of the Dance Band in the 1930s. Town Hall dances were very popular at that time.

Old Ashburnian Society reunion, 1970. Diana Walker presents a bouquet to the President's wife, Mrs A Froggatt, with Mrs Kimmins, Mr Kimmins (headmaster) and Mr A Froggatt.